From the library of

Herb Fam
Christmas 74
from Lena

Foreword for Songs from Green Pastures

"He makes me to lie down. . . ." The one who wrote these words also wrote, "My soul cleaveth unto the dust. . . ." Our pastures are not always green nor pleasant places to lie down and rest. However, we need to learn to sing new songs in the springtime pastures because we have survived the heart-breaking winters.

One of King David's prayers says, "Try me, prove me" (Ps. 26:2). It causes us to focus on the opportunities that exist in suffering—opportunities to stretch our faith and trust in God. Sometimes our pain, like David's, is so intense that all the Lord hears is our cries or our whispers, but He always listens. Just as the Lord delights in His intricate design for nature, so He also delights in our uniqueness.

In the secret places where we trust the Lord, there is hope—the hope King David saw— to give us confidence so we can sing praises when we reflect on the Lord's laws. What better combination could there be than nature's majesty coupled with the wisdom of the Psalms. In this book, the pictures and passages from the Psalms together with the prayers, show us how, regardless of the circumstances, we can "give thanks."

Songs from Green Pastures is a charming collection of nature's beauty in photography, the poetry of the Psalms, and heartfelt meditations. All the selections in this book are designed for you and for me—they describe our deepest needs and hurts. I pray that you will be inspired to walk in greener pastures after reading this special devotional, and "in everything give thanks."

by Ruth Bell Graham

PHOTOS BY:	PAGE:
Bavaria:	Front cover, 26, 48-49
Tony Stone:	3, 4-5, 14, 50, 56, 57, 78
Mauritius:	6-7, 15, 16-17, 24-25, 32-33
Rudolf Rauth:	8-9
Walter Studer:	10, 70, 71
R. Cushman Hayes:	11, 27, 43, 44, 45, 62, 63, 64-65, 74, 75
Willi Rauch:	12-13, 60, 61
Willi Burkhardt:	18-19, 20-21, 28-29, 40-41, 52-53, 66-67, 68-69, 76-77
Toni Schneiders:	22-23
Otto Pfenninger:	30-31, 72-73
Siegfried Eigstler:	36-37, 38-39, 46-47
Jørgen Vium Olesen:	42, 54, 55, 58, 59
Ben Alex:	51

Songs from Green Pastures
Daybreak Books are published by the Zondervan Publishing House
1415 Lake Drive, S.E., Grand Rapids, Michigan 49506
Copyright © 1988 by Forlaget Scandanavia
Noerregade 32, 1165, Copennagen K, Denmark

ISBN 0-310-54630-3

Edited by Jorgen Vium Olesen and Nia Jones
Text by Edith Schaeffer from *L'Abri,* and *Common Sense,*
Printed in Hong Kong by South Sea International Press Ltd.

SONGS FROM GREEN PASTURES

Selections from the Psalms with prayer meditations

Edited by Jørgen Vium Olesen and Nia Jones
Text by Edith Schaeffer
Scripture text from The Holy Bible, New International Version

Daybreak Books

Zondervan Publishing House
Grand Rapids, Michigan

*He makes me to
lie down in green
pastures; He leads me beside
the still waters. He restores my soul;
He leads me in the paths of
righteousness For His
name's sake.*

*I will bless
the Lord at all
times; His praise
shall continually be in
my mouth. My soul shall make
its boast in the Lord; The humble
shall hear of it and be glad. Oh, magnify
the Lord with me, And let us exalt
His name together. I sought the
Lord, and He heard me, And
delivered me from
all my
fears.*

The Laws of the Lord

By them is your servant warned; in keeping them there is great reward.

The heavens declare the glory og God; the skies proclaim the work of his hands.
Day efter day they pour forth speech; night after night they display knowledge.
There is no speech or language where their voice is not heard.
Their voice goes out into all the earth, their words to the ends of the world.

In the heavens he has pitched a tent for the sun, which is like a bridegroom coming forth from his pavilion, like a champion rejoicing to run his course.
It rises at one end of the heavens and makes its circuit to the other; nothing is hidden from it heat.

The law of the Lord is perfect, reviving the soul. The statutes of the Lord are trustworthy, making wise the simple.
The precepts of the Lord are right, giving joy to the heart. The commands of the Lord are radiant, giving light to the eyes.
The fear of the Lord is pure, enduring forever. The ordinances of the Lord are sure and altogether righteous.
They are more precious than gold, than much pure gold; they are sweeter than honey, than honey from the comb.
By them is your servant warned; in keeping them there is great reward.

Who can discern his errors? Forgive my hidden faults.
Keep your servant also from willful sins; may they not rule over me. Then will I be blameless, innocent of great transgression.
May the words of my mouth and the meditation of my heart be pleasing in your sight, O Lord, my Rock and my Redeemer.

God is utterly fair. He gave a very complete book for us to read and reread.

We Trust in the Power of God

*They are brought to their knees and fall, but we
rise up and stand firm.*

May the Lord answer you when you are in distress; may
the name of the God of Jacob protect you.
May he send you help from the sanctuary and grant you
support from Zion.
May he remember all your sacrifices and accept your
burnt offerings. — Selah
May he give you the desire of your heart and make all
your plans succeed.
We will shout for joy when you are victorious and will
lift up our banners in the name of our God. May the
Lord grant all your requests.
Now I know that the Lord saves his anointed; he
answers him from his holy heaven with the saving
power of his right hand.
Some trust in chariots and some in horses, but we trust
in the name of the Lord our God.
They are brought to their knees and fall, but we rise up
and stand firm.
O Lord, save the king! Answer us when we call!

*As we look back on it now, we had a
"preview" in those first two months, of
what was coming years later, but we had
no idea of that. We only knew that our
prayer for guidance had been answered,
and that our coming to Champéry had
far more purpose than just satisfying the
children's longing for a home, and for a
home in the charming "tucked in the
mountains" village which Champéry is.
We knew God had brought us there.*

God's Blessings

You have granted him the desire of his heart and have not withheld the request of his lips.

Lord, the king rejoices in your strength. How great is his joy in the victories you give?

You have granted him the desire of his heart and have not withheld the request of his lips.

You welcomed him with rich blessings and placed a crown of pure gold on his head.

He asked you for life, and you gave it to him — length of days, for ever and ever.

Through the victories you gave, his glory is great; you have bestowed on him splendor and majesty.

Surely you have granted him eternal blessings and made him glad with the joy of your presence.

For the king trusts in the Lord; through the unfailing love of the Most High he will not be shaken.

Your hand will lay hold on all your enemies; your right hand will seize your foes.

At the time of your appearing you will make them like a fiery furnace. In his wrath the Lord will swallow them up, and his fire will consume them.

You will destroy their descendants from the earth, their posterity from mankind. Though they plot evil against you and devise wicked schemes, they cannot succeed;

for you will make them turn their backs when you aim at them with drawn bow.

Be exalted, O Lord, in your strength; we will sing and praise your might.

So it was that the impossible happened. . . . We believe it was not "chance" or "luck," but a definite answer on the part of God.

Stay Near to Me

Do not be far from me, for trouble is near and there is no one to help.

My God, my God, why have you forsaken me? Why are you so far from saving me, so far from the words of my groaning?
O my God, I cry out by day but you do not answer, by night, and am not silent.

Yet you are enthroned as the Holy One; you are the praise of Israel.
In you our fathers put their trust; they trusted and you delivered them.
They cried to you and were saved; in you they trusted and were not disappointed.

But I am a worm and not a man, scorned by men and despised by the people.
All who see me mock me; they hurl insults, shaking their heads:
"He trusts in the Lord; let the Lord rescue him. Let him deliver him, since he delights in him."

Yet you brought me out of the womb; you made me trust in you even at my mother's breast.
From birth I was upon you; from my mother's womb you have been my God.
Do not be far from me, for trouble is near and there is no one to help.

Many bulls surround me; strong bulls of Bashan encircle me.
Roaring lions tearing their prey open their mouths wide against me.
I am poured out like water, and all my bones are out of joint. My heart has turned to wax; it has melted away within me.
My strength is dried up like a potsherd, and my tongue sticks to the roof of my mouth; you lay me in the dust of death.

The thing about real life is that important events don't announce themselves. . . . Usually something that is going to change your whole life is a memory before you can stop and be impressed about it. You don't usually have a chance to get excited about that sort of thing . . . ahead of time!

A Song of Praise

All rich of the earth will feast and worship; all who go down to the dust will kneel before him — those who cannot keep themselves alive.

Dogs have surrounded me; a band of evil men has encircled me, they have pierced my hands and my feet. I can count all my bones; people stare and gloat over me.

They divide my garments among them and cast lots for my clothing.

But you, O Lord, be not far off; O my Strength, come quickly to help me.

Deliver my life from the sword, my precious life from the power of the dogs.

Rescue me from the mouth of the lions; save me from the horns of the wild oxen.

I will declare your name to my brothers; in the congregation I will praise you.

You who fear the Lord, praise him! All you descendants of Jacob, honor him! Revere him, all you descendants of Israel?

For he has not despised or disdained the suffering of the afflicted one; he has not hidden his face from him but has listened to his cry for help.

From you comes my praise in the great assembly; before those who fear you will I fulfill my vows.

The poor will eat and be satisfied; they who seek the Lord will praise him — may your hearts live forever!

All the ends of the earth will remember and turn to the Lord, and all the families of the nations will bow down before him,

for dominion belongs to the Lord and he rules over the nations.

All the rich of the earth will feast and worship; all who go down to the dust will kneel before him — those who cannot keep themselves alive.

Posterity will serve him; future generations will be told about the Lord. They will proclaim his righteousness to a people yet unborn — for he has done it.

Jesus is declaring that there is Someone who is called the Holy Spirit, who so affects the lives of the people He enters that results can be seen, which can be compared to the things our eyes see, the sensations our senses feel, when we are standing in the midst of wind.

My Shepherd

Surely goodness and love will follow me all the days of my life, and I will dwell in the house of the Lord forever.

The Lord is my shepherd, I shall lack nothing.
He makes me lie down in green pastures, he leads me beside quiet waters,
he restores my soul. He guides me in paths of righteousness for his name's sake.
Even though I walk through the valley of the shadow of death, I will fear no evil, for you are with me; your rod and your staff, they comfort me.

You prepare a table before me in the presence of my enemies. You anoint my head with oil; my cup overflows.
Surely goodness and love will follow me all the days of my life, and I will dwell in the house of the Lord forever.

A Christian's life is dependent upon the reality of his having been born, and his having life ... the life of the Spirit now within him.

The World Belongs to God

Who may ascend the hill of the Lord? Who may stand in his holy place?

The earth is the Lord's and everything in it, the world, and all who live in it;
for he founded it upon the seas and established it upon the waters.
Who may ascend the hill of the Lord? Who may stand in his holy place?
He who has clean hands and a pure heart, who does not lift up his soul to an idol or swear by what is false.
He will receive blessing from the Lord and vindication from God his Savior.
Such is the generation of those who seek him, who seek your face, O God of Jacob. — Selah

Lift up your heads, O you gates; be lifted up, you ancient doors, that the King of glory may come in.
Who is he this King of glory? The Lord Almighty — he is the King of glory.

Does becoming a Christian ensure you a happy life? That depends on your definition of happiness. . . . The deep, real joy that comes with knowing you are in contact with the living God is something no one would exchange who has known it.

He guides me
in the right paths,
as he has
promised.

Teach Me Your Ways

Remember, O Lord, your great mercy and love, for they are from of old.

To you, O Lord, I lift up my soul;
in you I trust, O my God. Do not let me be put to shame, nor let my enemies triumph over me.
No one whose hope is in you will ever be put to shame, but they will be put to shame who are treacherous without excuse.

Show me your ways, O Lord, teach me your paths;
guide me in your truth and teach me, for you are God my Savior, and my hope is in you all day long.
Remember, O Lord, your great mercy and love, for they are from of old.
Remember not the sins of my youth and my rebellious ways; according to your love remember me, for you are good, O Lord.

"Oh, God, I do believe that Jesus died for me. Please don't ever let me flinch."

I Come to You for Safety

*Who, then, is the man that fears the Lord? He will
instruct him in the way chosen for him.*

Good and upright is the Lord; therefore he instructs
sinners in his ways.
He guides the humble in what is right and teaches them
his way.
All the ways of the Lord are loving and faithful for those
who keep the demands of his covenant.
For the sake of your name, O Lord, forgive my iniquity,
though it is great.
Who, then, is the man that fears the Lord? He will
instruct him in the way chosen for him.
He will spend his days in prosperity, and his descendants
will inherit the land.
The Lord confides in those who fear him; he makes his
covenant known to them.
My eyes are ever on the Lord, for only he will release
my feet from the snare.

Turn to me and be gracious to me, for I am lonely and
afflicted.
The troubles of my heart have multiplied; free me from
my anguish.
Look upon my affliction and my distress and take away
all my sins.
See how my enemies have increased and how fiercely
they hate me!
Guard my life and rescue me; let me not be put to
shame, for I take refuge in you. May integrity and
uprightness protect me, because my hope is in you.
Redeem Israel, O God, from all their troubles!

*Le Havre was flooded with brilliant
sunlight as we approached the docks, and
stood out like a study in buff, cream and
tan against a bright blue backdrop of
sky. When Franky, in my arms on the
upper deck, wanted to get down and
walk, it seemed a natural thing to let
him run around a bit. . . . It was the last
time he ever walked without a handicap!*

Your Faithfulness Leads Me

Test me, O Lord, and try me, examine my heart and my mind.

Vindicate me, O Lord, for I have led a blameless life; I have trusted in the Lord without wavering.

Test me, O Lord, and try me, examine my heart and my mind;

for your love is ever before me, and I walk continually in your truth.

I do not sit with deceitful men, nor do I consort with hypocrites;

I abhor the assembly of evildoers and refuse to sit with the wicked.

I wash my hands in innocence, and go about your altar, O Lord,

proclaiming aloud your praise and telling of all your wonderful deeds.

I love the house where you live, O Lord, the place where your glory dwells.

Do not take away my soul along with sinners or my life with bloodthirsty men,

in whose hands are wicked schemes, whose right hands are full of bribes.

But I lead a blameless life; redeem me and be merciful to me.

My feet stand on level ground; in the great assembly I will praise the Lord.

How could I know what to do? . . . I cried out to God silently, "Oh, show me what to do, God. Oh, Father, show what is best for Franky."

Trust in the Lord

*Wait for the Lord; be strong and take heart and
wait for the Lord.*

The Lord is my light and my salvation — whom shall I
fear? The Lord is the stronghold of my life — of whom
shall I be afraid?
When evil men advance against me to devour my flesh,
when my enemies and my foes attack me, they will
stumble and fall.
Though an army besiege me, my heart will not fear;
though war break out against me, even then will I be
confident.
One thing I ask of the Lord, this is what I seek: that I
may dwell in the house of the Lord all the days of my
life, to gaze upon the beauty of the Lord and to seek him
in his temple.
For in the day of trouble he will keep me safe in his
dwelling; he will hide me in the shelter of his tabernacle
and set me high upon a rock.
Then my head will be exalted above the enemies who
surround me; at his tabernacle will I sacrifice with shouts
of joy; I will sing and make music to the Lord.
Hear my voice when I call, O Lord; be merciful to me
and answer me.
My heart says of you, "Seek his face!" Your face, Lord,
I will seek.
Do not hide your face from me, do not turn your servant
away in anger; you have been my helper. Do not reject
me or forsake me, O God my Savior.
Though my father and mother forsake me, the Lord will
receive me.
Teach me your way, O Lord; lead me in a straight path
because of my oppressors.
Do not turn me over to the desire of my foes, for false
witnesses rise up against me, breathing out violence.
I am still confident of this: I will see the goodness of the
Lord in the land of the living.
Wait for the Lord; be strong and take heart and wait for
the Lord.

*"If God can turn a King's heart the way
He can turn the course of a river, surely
God can turn the decision of this doctor
in the direction that will be best for
Franky"; and as I asked God to do this,
I felt comforted and stopped trembling.*

A Prayer of Help

Praise be to the Lord, for he has heard my cry for mercy. The Lord is my strength and my shield.

To you I call, O Lord my Rock; do not turn a deaf ear to me. For if you remain silent, I will be like those who have gone down to the pit.

Hear my cry for mercy as I call to you for help, as I lift up my hands toward your Most Holy Place.

Do not drag me away with the wicked, with those who do evil, who speak cordially with their neighbors but harbor malice in their hearts.

Repay them for their deeds and for their evil work; repay them for what their hands have done and bring back upon them what they deserve.

Since they show no regard for the works of the Lord and what his hands have done, he will tear them down and never build them up again.

Praise be to the Lord, for he has heard my cry for mercy.

The Lord is my strength and my shield; my heart trusts in him, and I am helped. My heart leaps for joy and I will give thanks to him in song.

The Lord is the strength of his people, a fortress of salvation for his anointed one.

Save your people and bless your inheritance; be their shepherd and carry them forever.

Then those avalanches and floods descended suddenly upon us. . . . I propped my Bible up on the keys of the typewriter, and asked God to give me the help and comfort I needed.

The Voice of the Lord

The voice of the Lord is over the waters; the God of glory thunders, the Lord thunders over the mighty waters.

Ascribe to the Lord, O mighty ones, ascribe to the Lord glory and strength.
Ascribe to the Lord the glory due his name; worship the Lord in the splendor of his holiness.
The voice of the Lord is over the waters; the God of glory thunders, the Lord thunders over the mighty waters.
The voice of the Lord is powerful; the voice of the Lord is majestic.
The voice of the Lord breaks the cedars; the Lord breaks in pieces the cedars of Lebanon.
He makes Lebanon skip like a calf, Sirion like a young wild ox.
The voice of the Lord strikes with flashes of lightning.
The voice of the Lord shakes the desert; the Lord shakes the Desert of Kadesh.
The voice of the Lord twists the oaks and strips the forests bare. And in his temple all cry, "Glory!"

The Lord sits enthroned over the flood; the Lord is enthroned as King forever.
The Lord gives strength to his people; the Lord blesses his people with peace.

My feeling was one of excitement. I read it over again, and then again . . . then reached for my pencil and wrote in the margin: "Jan. '55, promise . . . Yes, L'Abri." For I had had the tremendous surge of assurance that although this had another basic meaning, it was being used by God to tell me Something.

Sing Praise

O Lord my God, I called to you for help and you healed me.

I will exalt you, O Lord, for you lifted me out of the depths and did not let my enemies gloat over me.
O Lord my God, I called to you for help and you healed me.
O Lord, you brought me up from the grave; you spared me from going down into the pit.

Sing to the Lord, you saints of his; praise his holy name. For his anger lasts only a moment, but his favor lasts a lifetime; weeping may remain for a night, but rejoicing comes in the morning.

When I felt secure, I said, "I will never be shaken."
O Lord, when you favored me, you made my mountain stand firm; but when you hid your face, I was dismayed.

To you, O Lord, I called; to the Lord I cried for mercy: "What gain is there in my destruction, in my going down into the pit? Will the dust praise you? Will it proclaim your faithfulness?
Hear, O Lord, and be merciful to me; O Lord be my help."

You turned my wailing into dancing; you removed my sackcloth and clothed me with joy,
that my heart may sing to you and not be silent. O Lord. my God, I will give you thanks forever.

It seemed to me that God was putting His hand on my shoulder in a very real way and that He was saying that there would be a work which would be His work, not ours, which man could not stop. I felt that this work was going to be L'Abri.

*I will always
thank the Lord;
I will never stop
praising him.*

A Prayer of Trust in God

In you, O Lord, I have taken refuge; let me never be put to shame.

In you, O Lord, I have taken refuge; let me never be put to shame; deliver me in your righteousness.
Turn your ear to me, come quickly to my rescue; be my rock of refuge, a strong fortress to save me.
Since you are my rock and my fortress, for the sake of your name lead and guide me.
Free me from the trap that is set for me, for you are my refuge.
Into your hands I commit my spirit; redeem me, O Lord, the God of truth.
I hate those who cling to worthless idols; I trust in the Lord.
I will be glad and rejoice in your love, for you saw my affliction and knew the anguish of my soul.
You have not handed me over to the enemy but have set my feet in a spacious place.

Be merciful to me, O Lord, for I am in distress; my eyes grow weak with sorrow, my soul and my body with grief.
My life is consumed by anguish and my years by groaning; my strength fails because of my affliction, and my bones grow weak.
Because of all my enemies, I am the utter contempt of my neighbors; I am a dread to my friends — those who see me on the street flee from me.
I am forgotten by them as though I were dead; I have become like broken pottery.
For I hear the slander of many; there is terror on every side; they conspire against me and plot to take my life.

"Oh, Heavenly Father, we want Thy plan, not our own; we want definite assurance that Thou are leading, . . ."

In Your Care

Be strong and take heart, all you who hope in the Lord.

But I trust in you, O Lord; I say, "You are my God."
My times are in your hands; deliver me from my
enemies and from those who pursue me.
Let your face shine on your servant; save me in your
unfailing love.
Let me not be put to shame, O Lord, for I have cried out
to you; but let the wicked be put to shame and lie silent
in the grave.
Let their lying lips be silenced, for with pride and
contempt they speak arrogantly against the righteous.

How great is your goodness, which you have stored up
for those who fear you, which you bestow in the sight of
men on those who take refuge in you.
In the shelter of your presence you hide them from the
intrigues of men; in your dwelling you keep them safe
from the strife of tongues.

Praise be to the Lord, for he showed his wonderful love
to me when I was in a besieged city.
In my alarm I said, "I am cut off from your sight!" Yet
you heard my cry for mercy when I called to you for
help.
Love the Lord, all his saints! The Lord preserves the
faithful, but the proud he pays back in full.
Be strong and take heart, all you who hope in the Lord.

*Do we believe God is able to do
something in government offices, in this
present situation, as He was able in
times past? Do we believe our God is the
God of Daniel? If so, we have an
opportunity to prove it now.*

I Will Instruct You

Rejoice in the Lord and be glad, you righteous; sing, all you who are upright in heart!

Blessed is he whose trangressions are forgiven, whose sins are covered.

Blessed is the man whose sin the Lord does not count against him and in whose spirit is no deceit.

When I kept silent, my bones wasted away through my groaning all day long.

For day and night your hand was heavy upon me; my strength was sapped as in the heat of summer.

Then I acknowledged my sin to you and did not cover up my iniquity. I said, "I will confess my transgressions to the Lord" — and you forgave the guilt of my sin.— Selah

Therefore let everyone who is godly pray to you while you may be found; surely when the mighty waters rise, they will not reach him.

You are my hiding place; you will protect me from trouble and surround me with songs of deliverance.—

Selah

I will instruct you and teach you in the way you should go; I will counsel you and watch over you.

Do not be like the horse or the mule, which have no understanding but must be controlled by bit and bridle or they will not come to you.

Many are the woes of the wicked, but the Lord's unfailing love surrounds the man who trusts in him.

Rejoice in the Lord and be glad, you righteous; sing, all you who are upright in heart!

The cold, sick, depressed feeling left me, and I was filled with a warmth of expectancy and faith that God was going to guide us, and that He could do the impossible and that He would show us the "way." I felt a great surge of thankfulness to Him for giving us an opportunity to really see Him work.

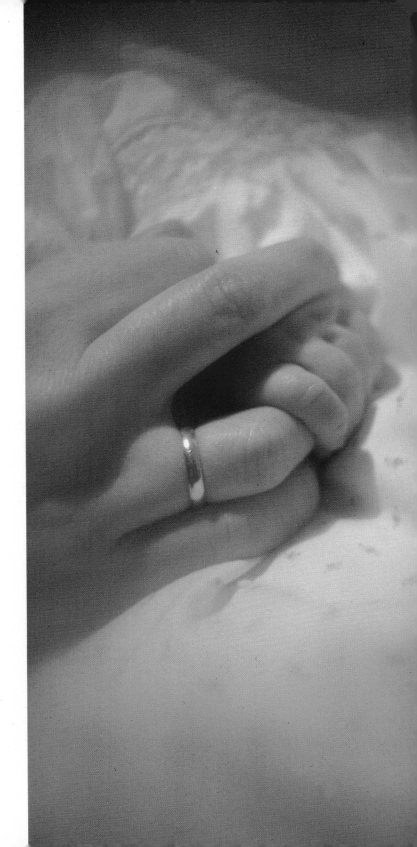

Sing a New Song

Let all the earth fear the Lord.

Sing joyfully to the Lord, you righteous; it is fitting for the upright to praise him.
Praise the Lord with the harp; make music to him on the ten-stringed lyre.
Sing to him a new song; play skillfully, and shout for joy.
For the word of the Lord is right and true; he is faithful in all he does.
The Lord loves righteousness and justice; the earth is full of his unfailing love.

By the word of the Lord were the heavens made, their starry host by the breath of his mouth.
He gathers the waters of the sea into jars; he puts the deep into storehouses.
Let all the earth fear the Lord; let all the people of the world revere him.
For he spoke, and it came to be; he commanded, and it stood firm.
The Lord foils the plans of the nations; he thwarts the purposes of the peoples.
But the plans of the Lord stand firm forever, the purposes of his heart through all generations.

Blessed is the nation whose God is the Lord, the people he chose for his inheritance.

"Oh, Heavenly Father . . . please show us today something of Thy power. Give us a sign of the fact that Thou are hearing us as we pray concerning this whole thing."

The Lord Watches Over Those Who Obey Him

*May your unfailing love rest upon us, O Lord, even
as we put our hope in you.*

From heaven the Lord looks down and sees all
mankind;
from his dwelling place he watches all who live on
earth —
he who forms the hearts of all, who considers everything
they do.
No king is saved by the size of his army; no warrior
escapes by his great strength.
A horse is a vain hope for deliverance; despite all its
great strength it cannot save.
But the eyes of the Lord are on those who fear him, on
those whose hope is in his unfailing love,
to deliver them from death and keep them alive in
famine.
We wait in hope for the Lord; he is our help and our
shield.
In him our hearts rejoice, for we trust in his holy name.
May your unfailing love rest upon us, O Lord, even as
we put our hope in you.

*We believed all this to be an answer to
prayer, on the part of a God who exists,
and who listens to His children when
they pray. . . .*

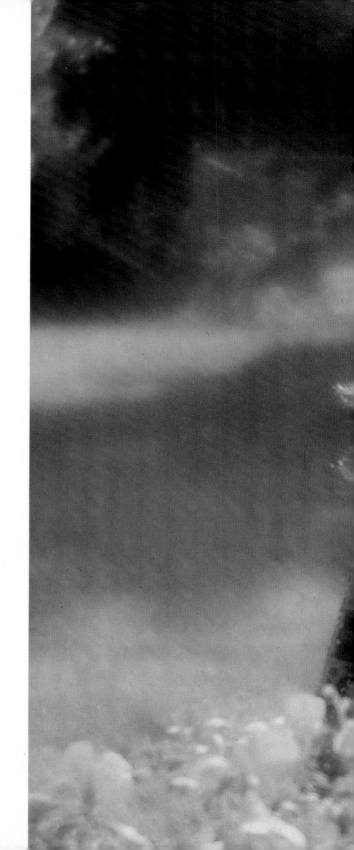

In Praise of God's Goodness

Glorify the Lord with me; let us exalt his name together.

I will extol the Lord at all times; his praise will always be on my lips.

My soul will boast in the Lord; let the afflicted hear and rejoice.

Glorify the Lord with me; let us exalt his name together.

I sought the Lord, and he answered me; he delivered me from all my fears.

Those who look to him are radiant; their faces are never covered with shame.

This poor man called, and the Lord heard him; he saved him out of all his troubles.

The angel of the Lord encamps around those who fear him, and he delivers them.

Taste and see that the Lord is good; Blessed is the man who takes refuge in him.

Fear the Lord, you his saints, for those who fear him lack nothing.

The lions may grow weak and hungry, but those who seek the Lord lack no good thing.

Come, my children, listen to me; I will teach you the fear of the Lord.

Whoever of you loves life and desires to see many good days,keep your tongue from evil and your lips from speaking lies.

Turn from evil and do good; seek peace and pursue it.

The eyes of the Lord are on the righteous and his ears are attentive to their cry;

God understands us. Although He is infinite, He understands our finiteness. Although He is unlimited, He understands our limitedness.

The Lord will Save His People

The Lord is close to the brokenhearted and saves those who are crushed in spirit.

The face of the Lord is against those who do evil, to cut off the memory of them from the earth.

The righteous cry out, and the Lord hears them; he delivers them from all their troubles.

The Lord is close to the brokenhearted and saves those who are crushed in spirit.

A righteous man may have many troubles, but the Lord delivers him from them all; he protects all his bones, not one of them will be broken.

Evil will slay the wicked; the foes of the righteous will be condemned.

The Lord redeems his servants; no one who takes refuge in him will be condemned.

God's way of doing things is the measuring stick given to us to measure ourselves by. We are not to use it to judge each other, but to stand directly alone before God and to check up, time after time, on whether or not we are sincerely and practically serving and with the right motives.

His anger lasts only a moment, his goodness for a lifetime.

There is No One Like You

*You rescue the poor from those too strong for
them, the poor and needy from those who rob
them.*

Contend, O Lord, with those who contend with me;
fight against those who fight against me.
Take up shield and buckler; arise and come to my aid.
Brandish spear and javelin against those who pursue
me.
Say to my soul, "I am your salvation."
May those who seek my life be disgraced and put to
shame; may those who plot my ruin be turned back in
dismay.
May they be like chaff before the wind, with the angel of
the Lord driving them away; may their path be dark and
slippery, with the angel of the Lord pursuing them.
Since they hid their net for me without cause and
without cause dug a pit for me,
may ruin overtake them by surprise — may the net they
hid entangle them, may they fall into the pit, to their
ruin.
Then my soul will rejoice in the Lord and delight in his
salvation.
My whole being will exclaim, "Who is like you, O Lord?
You rescue the poor from those too strong for them, the
poor and needy from those who rob them."

God the Father is personal to us. We
may come to Him privately, alone,
communicating directly to Him, talking to
Him in prayer with expressed love,
adoration, worship, praise, as well as
with requests. Because of His infiniteness
He can receive each of us as if we were
the only one praying at that time.

Rescue Me

I will give you thanks in the great assembly; among throngs of people I will praise you.

Ruthless witnesses come forward; they question me on things I know nothing about.
They repay me evil for good and leave my soul forlorn.
Yet when they were ill, I put on sackcloth and humbled myself with fasting. When my prayers returned to me unanswered,
I went about mourning as though for my friend or brother. I bowed my head in grief as though weeping for my mother.
But when I stumbled, they gathered in glee; attackers gathered against me when I was unaware. They slandered me without ceasing.
Like the ungodly they maliciously mocked; they gnashed their teeth at me.

O Lord, how long will you look on? Rescue my life from their ravages, my precious life from these lions.
I will give you thanks in the great assembly; among throngs of people I will praise you.

It is correct to sing, "Jesus loves me, this I know, for the Bible tells me so."

How Great is the Lord

*My tongue will speak of your righteousness and of
your praises all day long.*

Let not those gloat over me who are my enemies
without cause; let not those who hate me without reason
maliciously wink the eye.
They do not speak peaceably, but devise false accusa-
tions against those who live quietly in the land.
They gape at me and say, "Aha! Aha! With our own
eyes we have seen it."
O Lord, you have seen this; be not silent. Do not be far
from me, O Lord.
Awake, and rise to my defense! Contend for me, my
God and Lord.
Vindicate me in your righteousness, O Lord my God;
do not let them think, "Aha, just what we wanted!" or
say, "We have swallowed him up."

May all who gloat over my distress be put to shame and
confusion; may all who exalt themselves over me be
clothed with shame and disgrace.
May those who delight in my vindication shout for joy
and gladness; may they always say, "The Lord be
exalted, who delights in the well-being of his servant."
My tongue will speak of your righteousness and of your
praises all day long.

*Common sense Christian living, in the
framework God Himself has given, is the
path to life now, as God means it to be.*

The Source of All Life

For with you is the fountain of life; in your light we see light.

An oracle is within my heart concerning the sinfulness of the wicked: There is no fear of God before his eyes.
For in his own eyes he flatters himself too much to detect or hate his sin.
The words of his mouth are wicked and deceitful; he has ceased to be wise and to do good.
Even on his bed he plots evil; he commits himself to a sinful course and does not reject what is wrong.

Your love, O Lord, reaches to the heavens, your faithfulness to the skies.
Your righteousness is like the mighty mountains, your justice like the great deep. O Lord, you preserve both man and beast.
How priceless is your unfailing love! Both high and low among men find refuge in the shadow of your wings.
They feast on the abundance of your house; you give them drink from your river of deligths.
For with you is the fountain of life; in your light we see ligth.
Continue your love to those who know you, your righteousness to the upright in heart.
May the foot of the proud not come against me, nor the hand of the wicked drive me away.
See how the evildoers lie fallen — thrown down, not able to rise!

In the very midst of the most difficult times filled with anxiety, God has given us His pattern for the continuity of our relationship with Him. He does not leave us without explanation of what to do.

Trust in the Lord and Do Good

Trust in the Lord and do good; dwell in the land and enjoy safe pasture. Delight yourself in the Lord and he will give you the desires of your heart.

Do not fret because of evil men or be envious of those who do wrong;
for like the grass they will soon wither, like green plants they will soon die away.

Trust in the Lord and do good; dwell in the land and enjoy safe pasture.

Delight yourself in the Lord and he will give you the desires of your heart.

Commit your way to the Lord; trust in him and he will do this:

He will make your righteousness shine like the dawn, the justice of your cause like the noonday sun.

Be still before the Lord and wait patiently for him; do not fret when men succeed in their ways, when they carry out their wicked schemes.

Refrain from anger and turn from wrath; do not fret—it leads only to evil.

For evil men will be cut off, but those who hope in the Lord will inherit the land.

A little while, and the wicked will be no more; though you look for them, they will not be found.

But the meek will inherit the land and enjoy great peace.

The wicked plot against the righteous and gnash their teeth at them;

but the Lord laughs at the wicked, for he knows their day is coming.

The wicked draw the sword and bend the bow to bring down the poor and needy, to slay those whose ways are upright.

But their swords will pierce their own hearts, and their bows will be broken.

He is our refuge and strength; a very present *help in trouble. Our help is to come from Him as we run into the shelter of His arms, away from the noise of the battle, or the storm. He has promised us comfort, and we need to climb on His lap as a weeping, hurt child, not to kick at Him.*

The Lord Protects Those Who Please Him

The Lord delights in the way of the man whose steps he has made firm; though he stumble, he will not fall, for the Lord upholds him with his hand.

Better the little that the righteous have than the wealth of many wicked;
for the power of the wicked will be broken, but the Lord upholds the righteous.
The days of of the blameless are known to the Lord, and their inheritance will endure forever.
In times of disaster they will not wither; in days of famine they will enjoy plenty.
But the wicked will perish: The Lord's enemies will be like the beauty of the fields, they will vanish—vanish like smoke.
The wicked borrow and do not repay, but the righteous give generously;
those the Lord blesses will inherit the land, but those he curses will be cut off.
The Lord delights in the way of man whose steps he has made firm;
though he stumble, he will not fall, for the Lord upholds him with his hand.
I was young and now I am old, yet I have never seen the righteous forsaken or their children begging bread.
They are always generous and lend freely; their children will be blessed.

Constantly during the day we need to verbalize to the Lord our expressions of love, dwelling on the reasons for that love, whether it is the titanic reason of His providing eternal life, or the recognition of the wonder of His design of the first snowdrop or violet found in the woods in the spring.

Put Your Hope in the Lord

*Consider the blameless, observe the upright; there
is a future for the man of peace.*

Turn from evil and do good; then you will always live
securely.
For the Lord loves the just and will not forsake his
faithful ones.
They will be protected forever, but the offspring of the
wicked will be cut off;
the righteous will inherit the land and dwell in it forever.
The mouth of the righteous man utters wisdom and his
tongue speaks what is just.
The law of his God is in his heart; his feet do not slip.
The wicked lie in wait for the righteous, seeking their
very lives;
but the Lord will not leave them in their power or let
them be condemned when brought to trial.
Wait for the Lord and keep his way. He will exalt you to
possess the land; when the wicked are cut off, you will
see it.
I have seen a wicked and ruthless man flourishing like a
green tree in its native soil,
but he soon passed away and was no more; though I
looked for him, he could not be found.
Consider the blameless, observe the upright; there is a
future for the man of peace.
But all sinners will be destroyed; the future of the
wicked will be cut off.
The salvation of the righteous comes from the Lord; he
is their stronghold in time of trouble.
The Lord helps them and delivers them; he delivers
them from teh wicked and saves them, because they
take refuge in him.

*With David, we, in our own century, our
moment of history, are to verbalize with
our lips our satisfaction with our
compassionate and wonderful God. . . .
We are to trust Him by verbalizing that
trust and to love Him by expressing that
love.*

*The world
and all that is in it
belong to the Lord; the earth
and all who live on it
are his.*

The Prayer of a Suffering Man

All my longings lie open before you, O Lord; my sighing is not hidden from you.

O Lord, do not rebuke me in your anger or discipline me in your wrath.

For your arrows have pierced me, and your hand has come down upon me.

Because of your wrath there is no health in my body; my bones have no soundness because of my sin.

My guilt has overwhelmed me like a burden too heavy to bear.

My wounds fester and are loathsome because of my sinful folly.

I am bowed down and brought very low; all day long I go about mourning.

My back is filled with searing pain; there is no health in my body.

I am feeble and utterly crushed; I groan in anguish of heart.

All my longings lie open before you, O Lord; my sighing is not hidden from you.

My heart pounds, my strength fails me; even the light has gone from my eyes.

My friends and companions avoid me because of my wounds; my neighbors stay far away.

God tells us what He does not change. He will be tomorrow as He was yesterday. We can depend on Him to be faithful, reliable, trustworthy.

My God Will Help Me

I wait for you, O Lord; you will answer, O Lord my God.

Those who seek my life set their traps, those who would harm me talk of my ruin; all day long they plot deception.

I am like a deaf man, who cannot hear, like a mute, who cannot open his mouth;

I have become like a man who does not hear, whose mouth can offer no reply.

I wait for you, O Lord; you will answer, O Lord my God.

For I said, "Do not let them gloat or exalt themselves over me when my foot slips."

For I am about to fall, and my pain is ever with me.

I confess my iniquity; I am troubled by my sin.

Many are those who are my vigorous enemies; those who hate me without reason are numerous.

Those who repay my good with evil slander me when I seek what is good.

O Lord, do not forsake me; be not far from me, O my God.

Come quickly to help me, O Lord my Savior.

God is not ashamed to be called our God in times of distress, depression, despair, shipwrecks, sudden attacks of terrorists, cancer, fire, airplane crashes, because He knows there is an unbroken continuity ahead of us.

Hope in Suffering

But now, Lord, what do I loom for? My hope is in you.

I said, "I will watch my ways and keep my tongue from sin; I will put a muzzle on my mouth as long as the wicked are in my presence."
But when I was silent and still, not even saying anything good, my anguish increased.
My heart grew hot within me, and as I meditated, the fire burned; then I spoke with my tongue:

"Show me, O Lord, my life's end and the number of my days; let me know how fleeting is my life.
You have made my days a mere handbreadth; the span of my years is as nothing before you. Each man's life is but a breath.— Selah

Man is a mere phantom as he goes to and fro: He bustles about, but only in vain; he heaps up wealth, not knowing who will get it.

"But now, Lord, what do I look for? My hope is in you. Save me from all my transgressions; do not make me the scorn of fools.
I was silent; I would not open my mouth, for you are the one who has done this.
Remove your scourge from me; I am overcome by the blow of your hand.
You rebuke and discipline men for their sin; you consume their wealth like a moth — each man is but a breath.— Selah

"Hear my prayer, O Lord, listen to my cry for help; be not deaf to my weeping. For I dwell with you as an alien, a stranger, as all my fathers were.
Look away from me, that I may rejoice again before I depart and am no more."

Eternal life is for later in the perfection that will be God's future for us. But—at present—God's words to us in His Word are profoundly important and urgent.

The Lord created
the heavens by his command,
the sun, moon, and stars by his
spoken word.

Rejoice in the Lord,
O you righteous! For praise
from the upright is beautiful. Praise
the Lord with the harp; Make melody to Him
with an instrument of ten strings. Sing
to Him a new song; Play skillfully
with a shout of joy.